Adam Frost

THE
WESOME
BOOK OF
WESOMENESS

Illustrated by Dan Bramall

Published 2014 by Bloomsbury Publishing Plc
50 Bedford Square, London, WC1B 3DP
www.bloomsbury.com
Bloomsbury is a registered trademark of Bloomsbury Publishing Plc

9781408851180

A CIP record for this book is available from the British Library.

Printed in China by Leo Paper Products, Heshan, Guangdong

1 3 5 7 9 10 8 6 4 2

All figures used in this book are believed to be the latest and most accurate figures at
the point of publication unless the copy states otherwise. Where figures are estimates
or approximations, we have tried to make this clear. A selection of books and websites
we used for our facts can be found on the Sources page at the back of the book.

HARD TO STOMACH

We all swallow bits of hair and fluff every day without even noticing. But some people also chew their own hair, especially when they're bored. With gruesome consequences...

 Apple 6.3cm

DVD 12cm

 Hedgehog 20cm

Football 22cm

Largest ever hairball
38.1cm x 17.8cm

In November 2011, doctors at Rush University Medical Center in the United States removed a 10lb hairball from a woman's stomach. It measured 38.1cm x 17.8cm x 17.8cm.

I'LL EAT ANYTHING, ME

The strangest things ever found in a shark's stomach.

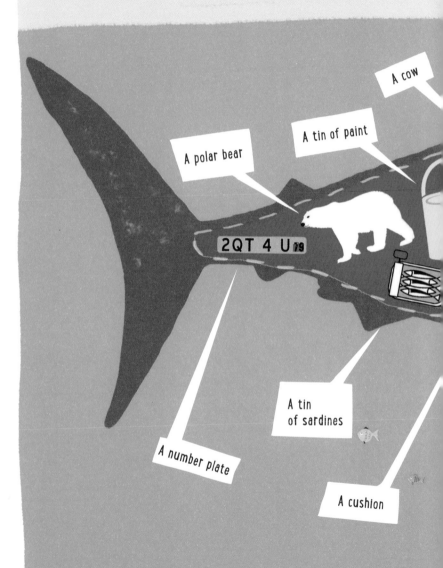

A cow

A tin of paint

A polar bear

2QT 4 U

A number plate

A tin of sardines

A cushion

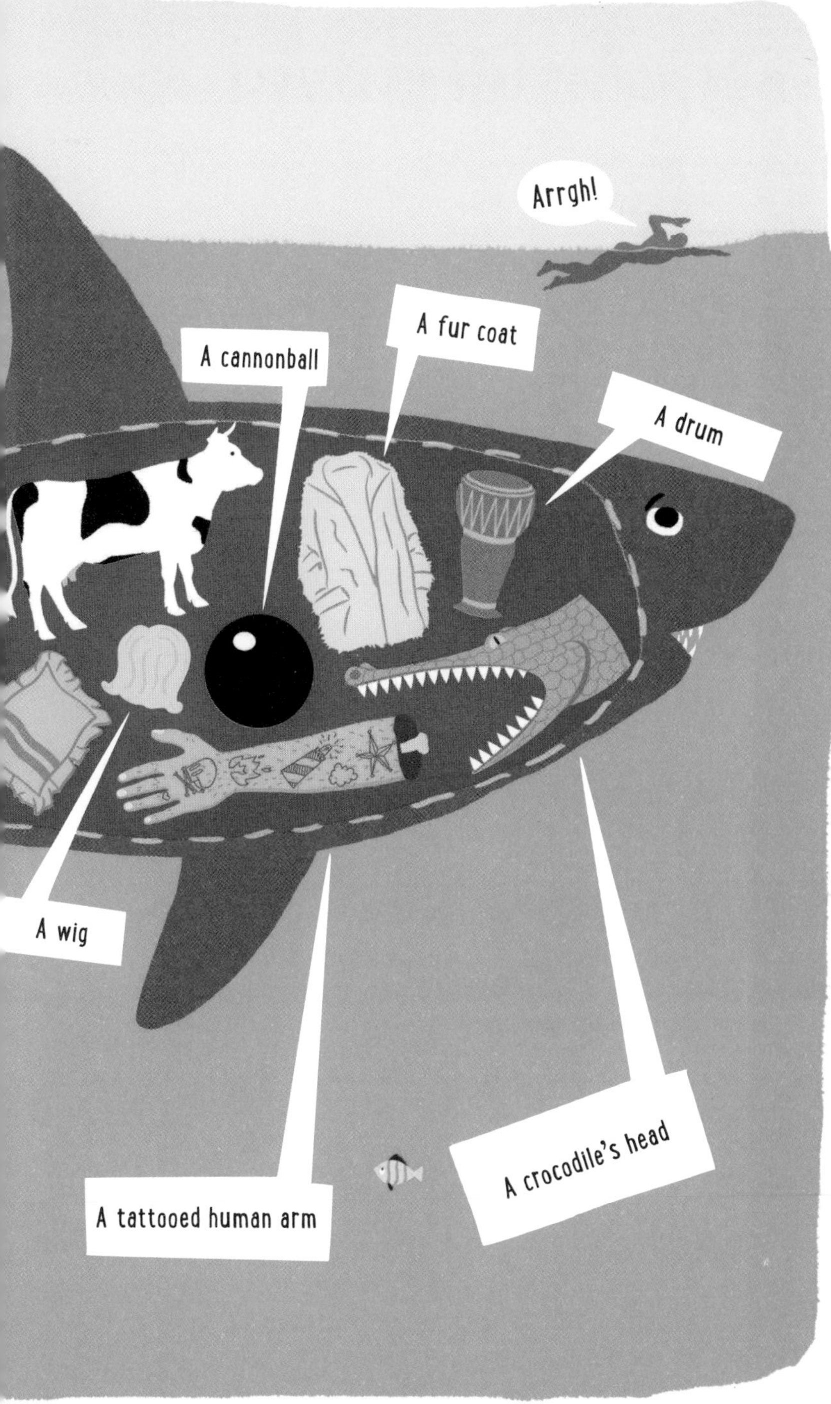
Arrgh!
A fur coat
A cannonball
A drum
A wig
A tattooed human arm
A crocodile's head

SURF'S UP

How big was the biggest wave ever recorded?

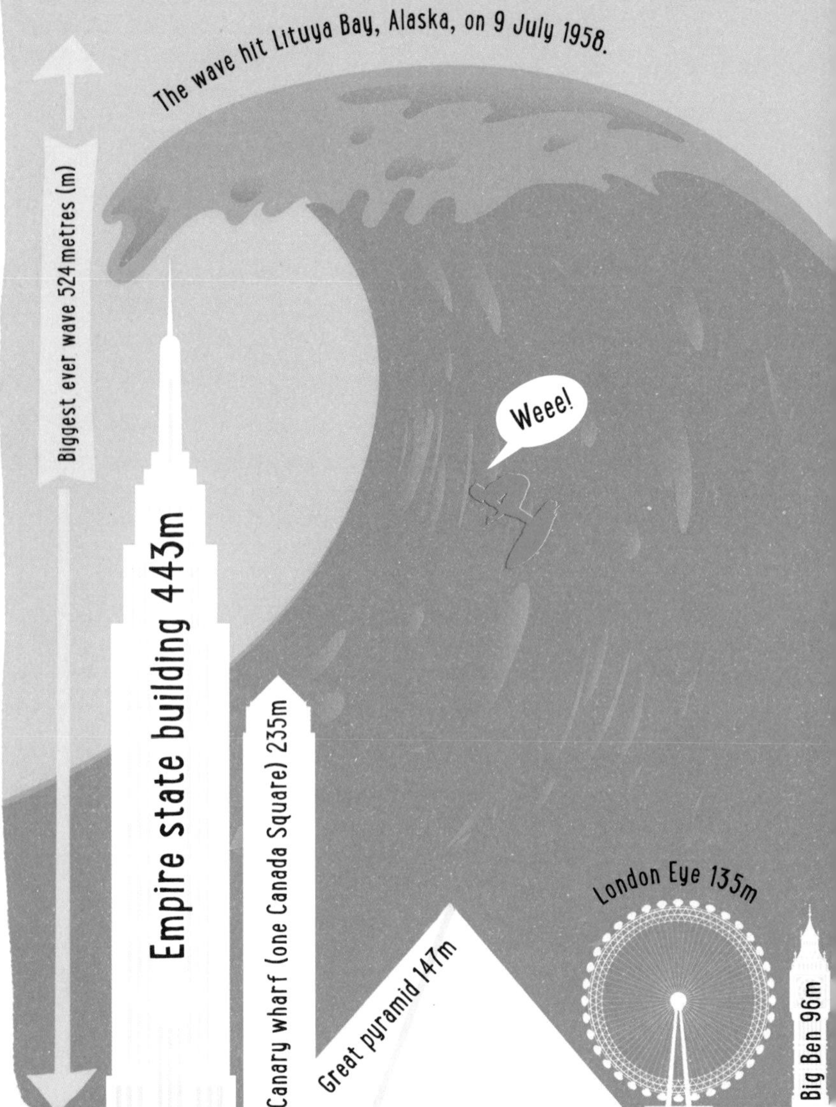

SNOT FUNNY

You swallow a litre
of snot every day.
So how much do you drink...

In a week?

Sink full
of snot

Fish tank full
of snot

In a month?

In three months?

Bath full of snot

In a year?

Paddling pool full of snot

FANGS A LOT

If a vampire fed on one person every day, and that person also became a vampire, here's what would happen...

Day Seven

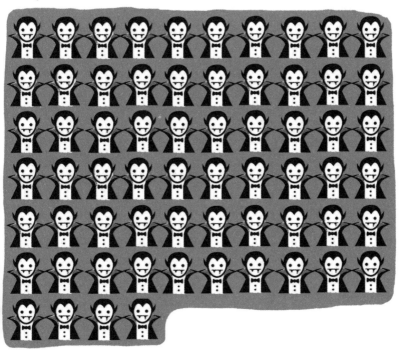

Day Eight

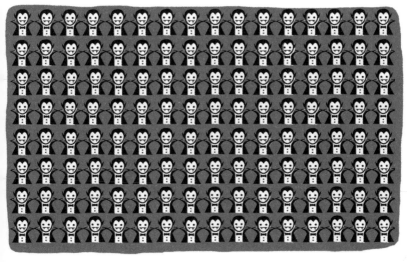

Day 27

Everyone in Britain is a vampire.

Day 32

Everyone in the world is a vampire.

A NEW LEAF

One of the oldest living things on Earth is a 4,767-year-old tree known as Methuselah. So what's happened on the planet since it started growing?

2560 BC
Great Pyramid completed

2832 BC
Methuselah starts to grow

1700 BC
Mammoth becomes extinct

2000 BC
Stonehenge completed

51 BC
Cleopatra becomes Queen of Egypt

Nearly 5,000 years later, Methuselah is still here.

79AD
Vesuvius erupts, burying Pompeii

1492
Christopher Columbus discovers America

Hello!

1969
Man lands on the moon

A BIT DENSE

In some countries it can get a bit crowded...

Singapore

19,863
people per square mile

Bangladesh

2,678
people per square mile

UK

679
people per square mile

Canada

10
people per square mile

NEED A LIFT?

The average man can lift around 58kg – which is roughly his own
bodyweight. Sounds impressive until you look at how animals measure u

A dung beetle can pull **1,141** times
its own bodyweight.

That's like **YOU** pulling
two fire engines along.

A rhinoceros beetle can lift **850**
times its own weight.

That's like **YOU** lifting up
three elephants.

A leafcutter ant can lift **50** times its own bodyweight with its jaws.

That's like **YOU** picking up a car with your teeth.

Rah!

A gorilla can lift **20** times its own bodyweight.

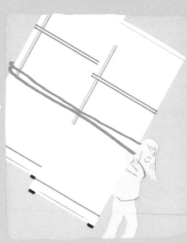

That's like **YOU** carrying two fridges.

NEED FOR SPEED

What's the fastest you can go in some places in different countries (in miles per hour)?

50 Vietnam

50 Iceland

70 UK

80 USA (on one highway in Texas)

80 Poland

NONE Germany

ZOOM!
ZOOM!

WIND POWER

The loudest burp ever was expelled by Paul Hunn of the UK in August 2009. Burps and other noises are measured in decibels.

HAIRDRYER
70 DECIBELS

ALARM CLOCK
80 DECIBELS

MOTORBIKE
95 DECIBELS

ELECTRIC DRILL
100 DECIBELS

LAWN MOWER
105 DECIBELS

LOUDEST BURP EVER
109.9 DECIBELS

RAINBOW BLOOD

Living things have different coloured blood. But what colour?

 **Red**

 Humans and most animals

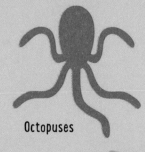 Octopuses

 Crabs/Lobsters

 Blue

Green

Samkos bush frog

Sea cucumber

Yellow

Clear

Spiders and some insects

WATER, WATER EVERYWHERE?

Almost three quarters of our planet is water.
But how much can we use?

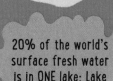

20% of the world's surface fresh water is in ONE lake: Lake Baikal in Russia.

Another 20% of the world's fresh water is in ONE river: the Amazon in South America.

The world's water:

97%
completely undrinkable (sea water)

2%
frozen in icebergs.

Less than 1%
usable by people.

Of the rest, a huge percentage has already been polluted by humans.

KING OF BLING

The largest ever gemstone yet found is a 536 kilograms (kg) emerald displayed in Hong Kong in 2009.

536kg

536kg is the same weight as seven men.

Diamonds are the most valuable gemstones. In 2010, a tiny pink diamond (just over 1cm wide) was bought for £29 million ($46 million).

With £29 million you could buy:

A private jet

Ten luxury yachts

120 houses

NO BUSINESS LIKE THROW BUSINESS

Since the dawn of time. human beings have thrown things at other human beings. But how far? And what weapons have they used?

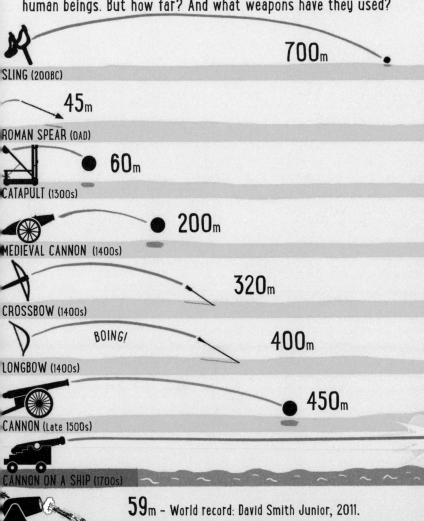

700m

SLING (200BC)

45m

ROMAN SPEAR (0AD)

60m

CATAPULT (1300s)

200m

MEDIEVAL CANNON (1400s)

320m

CROSSBOW (1400s)

BOING!

400m

LONGBOW (1400s)

450m

CANNON (Late 1500s)

CANNON ON A SHIP (1700s)

59m – World record: David Smith Junior, 2011.

MAN SHOT FROM CANNON (2000s)

SAY WHAT?

Some animals' names don't exactly make sense.

Woof!

A **prairie dog** is not a dog. It is a rodent.

A **flying fox** is not a fox. It is a bat.

A **polecat** is not a cat. It's more like a weasel.

A **horned toad** is not a toad. It's not even an amphibian. It's a lizard.

A **mongoose** is not a goose. It's more like a ferret.

1.6km

A **flying lemur**
can't fly and it isn't a lemur.

An **oystercatcher**
doesn't catch oysters. It prefers mussels and other shellfish.

A **white rhino** is
a rhino. But it isn't white. Not even a bit. It's grey.

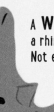

A **sea monkey** is
not a monkey. It's a type of shrimp.

Anteaters do occasionally eat ants. But they much prefer termites.

AND FINALLY... *Oink*

A **guinea pig** is not from
Guinea and it's definitely NOT a pig.

HOW MANY MAMMALS?

In the last Census, there were 63 million people living in the UK. But what if we'd included every mammal, not just humans?*

Horses
1 million

Dee
1 milli

Guinea Pigs
1 million

Voles
100 million

Around a quarter of all mammals in the UK are voles.

Bats
4.9 million

Sheep
32 million

Shrews
54 million

People
63 million

Cats
8 million

Rats
6.8 million

Squeak!

*This is based on the latest government information. Usually they count animals in the winter.

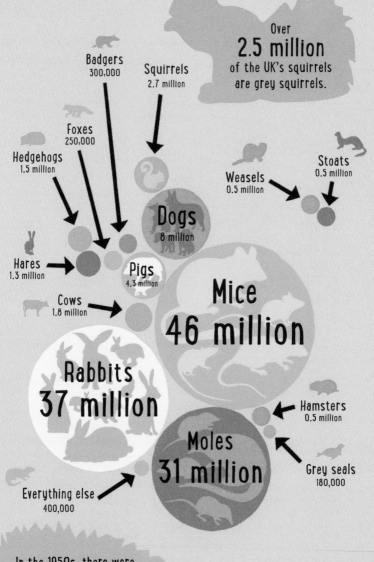

Over **2.5 million** of the UK's squirrels are grey squirrels.

Badgers
300,000

Squirrels
2.7 million

Foxes
250,000

Hedgehogs
1.5 million

Weasels
0.5 million

Stoats
0.5 million

Dogs
8 million

Hares
1.3 million

Pigs
4.3 million

Cows
1.8 million

**Mice
46 million**

**Rabbits
37 million**

Hamsters
0.5 million

**Moles
31 million**

Grey seals
180,000

Everything else
400,000

In the 1950s, there were
36 MILLION
hedgehogs in the UK.

IT CAME FROM OUTER SPACE

Two billion years ago. one of the largest
meteors ever to hit Earth landed in
Vredfort, South Africa. It created
the world's biggest crater.

The meteor
was travelling at
36,000 kmh*
(22,370 mph**).

It was twice as big
as the meteor that
supposedly killed off
the dinosaurs.

RUN!

*kilometres per hour **miles per hour

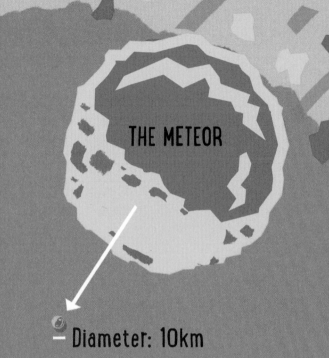

THE METEOR

Diameter: 10km

VREDFORT CRATER
Diameter: 300km

It would have caused a 1,000 megaton blast of energy.

Wait for me!

HOT STUFF

The Sun's energy is terrifying.

If you took exactly
THIS MUCH...

of the Sun's energy...

...and placed it
in the middle
of London

...everyone in
THAT CIRCLE
would be
DEAD!

London

France

PLANE CRAZY

In 1972, Vesna Vulovic fell 10,160m
from an aeroplane and survived...

But how far exactly is 10,160m?

Vesna Vulovic
10,160m

Mount Everest
8,848m

Bald Eagle
4,500m

Average skydiving height
4000m
(Unlike Vesna Vulovic,
skydivers have parachutes!)

Cumulus clouds
1,000m

World's tallest building
(Burj Khalifa)
830m

MOSTLY ARMLESS

Think you need a pair of hands to pick things up? Think again. Dong Changsheng pulled a 1500kg car 10m with his eyelids in 2006.

LAWS YOU MIGHT NOT KNOW

Here are some laws you've probably never heard of...

In Iceland, everyone has to learn to swim by law.

In Russia, it is illegal to brush your teeth more than twice a day.

In London, it is against the law to jump the queue in a tube station.

In Samoa, it is illegal for a man to forget his wife's birthday.

In Oklahoma, USA, it is illegal to pull faces at a dog.

In the UK, you are not allowed to handle salmon suspiciously.

In Thailand, it is against the law to leave the house with no underwear on.

In Portugal, it is illegal to wee in the sea.

In the UK, it is illegal to enter the Houses of Parliament wearing a suit of armour.

NATURAL BORN KILLERS

Many animals are deadly to humans. But which are the deadliest?

Each individual animal has enough venom in them to kill...

Inland taipan

100 people ✳

Box jellyfish

60 people ✳

Pufferfish

30 people

Blue ringed octopus

25 people

Cobra

20 people ✳

Cone snail

20 people

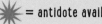

✳ = antidote available

GO GO GO!

How often do different animals need to poo?

one week

Sloth
On average, one poo a week.

Human
On average, one poo a day.

Poo!

Horse
Around ten poos a day.

Goose
One poo every 12 minutes,
or around 60 poos a day.

SLEEP TIGHT

How much sleep do animals need each night?

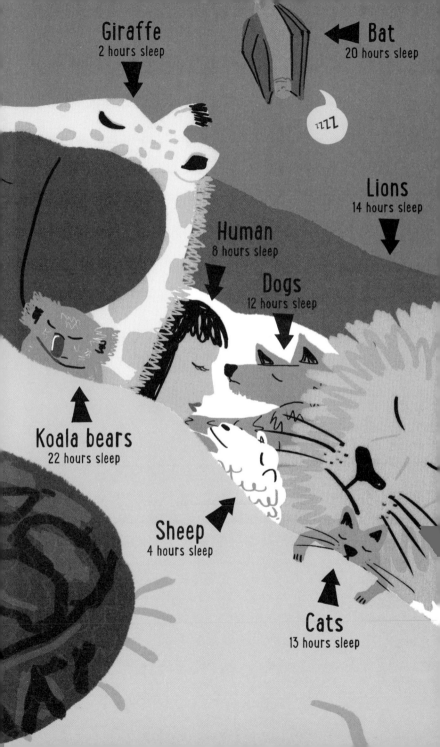

SIGHT FOR SORE EYES

As cities grow in size, air pollution can be an eye-wateringly large problem.

In 1940, visibility in Mexico City was 62 miles.

In 2000, visibility in Mexico City was one mile.

WHAT A LOAD OF RUBBISH!

There are millions of pieces of space junk in the atmosphere, caused by satellites crashing, rockets disintegrating, weapons exploding and a hundred other causes.

22,000
pieces of space junk are more than 10cm wide.

The weirdest is a spanner dropped from the International Space Station.

The biggest is the size of a washing machine.

Almost two-thirds
of the most dangerous space junk was created by explosions: a satellite being blown up in 2007 and two satelittes colliding in 2009.

Oh no!

Most space junk travels at
4.5 miles per second or roughly
16,200mph.

A single fleck of paint travelling
at this speed can cause
the same damage as a

**grand piano
travelling
at
60mph.**

The International Space Station
has to constantly steer
round space junk.

On average, a piece
of space junk falls
to Earth every day.
Nobody has been hit by
space junk... yet!

HEAVY LIFTING

The largest plane in the world, the An-225, was originally designed to lift the Russian space shuttle. Now it's used as a cargo plane in the Ukraine.

The An-225 can carry **300,000kg** of fuel. That could fill the tanks of 7,500 cars!

Fasten your seatbelts.

32 landing wheels

A An-225 plane holds the record for the largest ever amount of cargo:

253,820kg

That's like carrying a herd of

36 elephants.

88.4m wingspan

6 engines

THAT'S A WRAP!

It took 375 square metres (or 4,000 square feet) of bandages to make a mummy.

Tennis court
261m² (square metres)

Sheet for super king size bed
8.1m²

A saltwater crocodile
6.3m

A (very large) python
10m

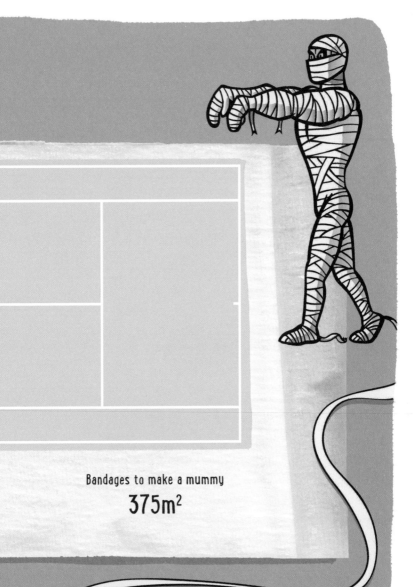

Bandages to make a mummy
375m²

The longest bandage used to wrap a mummy!
15m

LET US PREY

The rabbit is thought to be the most preyed-on animal in the world. Here's a selection of the predators that have it in for rabbits.

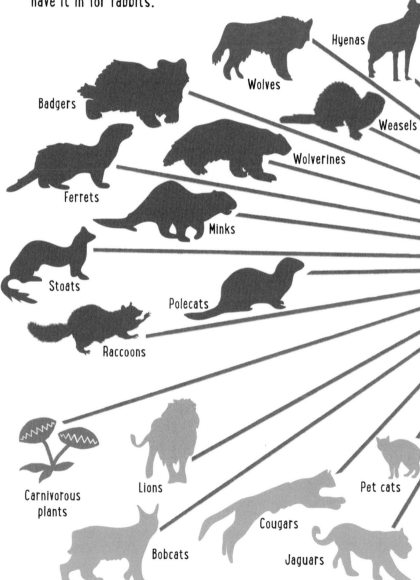

Foxes

Hyenas

Wolves

Weasels

Badgers

Wolverines

Ferrets

Minks

Stoats

Polecats

Raccoons

Carnivorous plants

Lions

Pet cats

Bobcats

Cougars

Jaguars

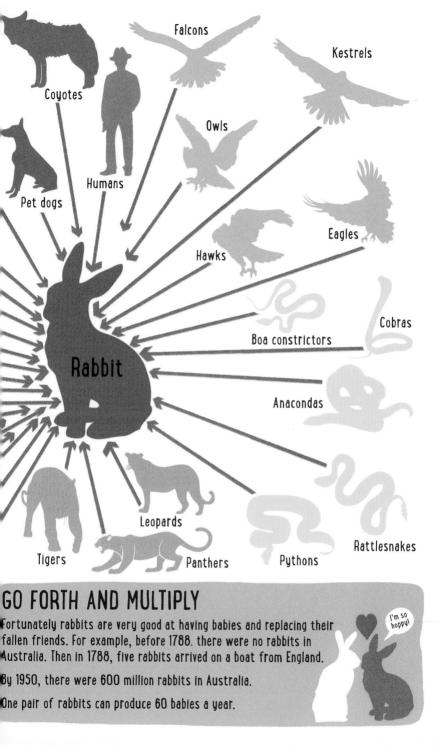

Coyotes

Falcons

Kestrels

Humans

Owls

Pet dogs

Hawks

Eagles

Cobras

Boa constrictors

Rabbit

Anacondas

Leopards

Rattlesnakes

Tigers

Panthers

Pythons

GO FORTH AND MULTIPLY

Fortunately rabbits are very good at having babies and replacing their fallen friends. For example, before 1788. there were no rabbits in Australia. Then in 1788, five rabbits arrived on a boat from England.

By 1950, there were 600 million rabbits in Australia.

One pair of rabbits can produce 60 babies a year.

I'm so hoppy!

STINGING IN THE RAIN

Many weird animals and objects have fallen
from the skies, including jellyfish...

Pennies and half pennies.
Hanham, UK, 1966

Snakes.
Tennessee, USA, 1877

Jellyfish.
Bath, UK, 1894

Worms.
Jennings, Louisiana, 2007

Ow!

Golfballs.
Florida, USA, 1969

Spiders.
Salta Province, Argentina, 2007

Orange snow.
Siberia, Russia, 2012

Frogs.
Ishikawa Prefecture,
Japan, 2009

Dead birds.
Faenza, Italy, 2011

Red rain.
Kerala, India, 2012

Fish.
Philippines, 2012

Diamonds.
OK, this has never
happened on Earth.
But scientists
believe that it rains
diamonds on both
Uranus and
Neptune!

UNDER PRESSURE

As you get deeper in the sea, the water around you puts more pressure on your body. But how much?

214m
Furthest ever reached by a freediver (i.e. someone just taking a deep breath). The pressure shrinks their lungs to the size of lemons.

2,500m
The pressure here is what your little toe would feel like if a hippo stood on it. But on every inch of your body.

3,784m
The wreck of the Titanic is here. According to one diver, the water pressure makes it look like it's been squashed by a giant's fist.

5,000m

Anglerfish and cusk eels live near the sea bed. They have adapted to avoid being crushed by the water around them. For example, the anglerfish has a skeleton made of cartilage (which is flexible and squeezable) rather than bone (which isn't).

200m

700m

A modern submarine has a 'crush depth' of about 700 metres. This is when the water pressure will start to crush its metal sides.

1,000m

1,900m

The deepest a whale can dive.

4,000m

Glugg!

4,000m

Here the pressure is almost 6,000 lbs per square inch. That's like being crushed alive in the jaws of a T Rex.

6,000m

10,000m

At the bottom of the sea, the pressure is like having 50 jumbo jets on top of you.

10,000m

RAIN CHECK

In 2005, Mumbai had 94cm of rain in a single day – the most ever recorded. But how much is 94cm?

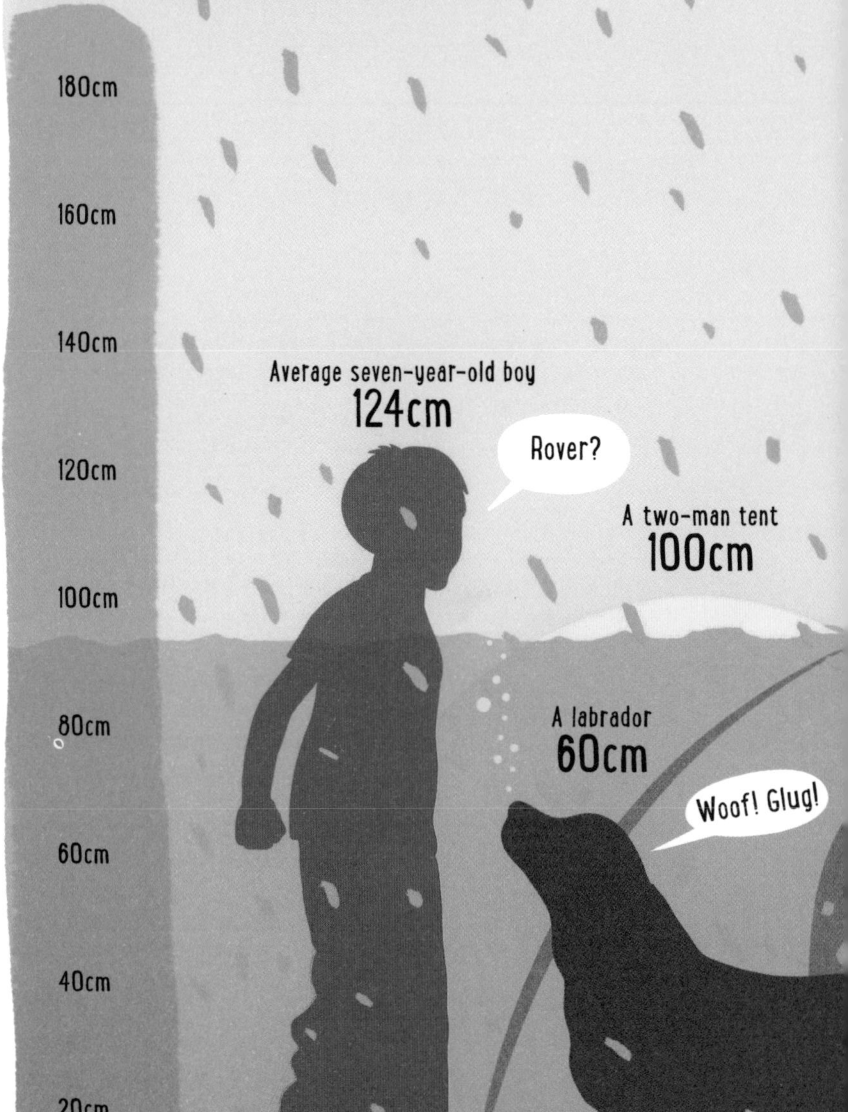

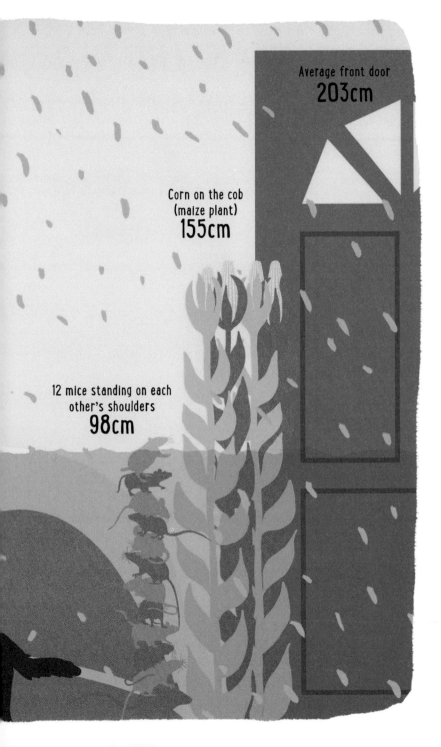

Average front door
203cm

Corn on the cob
(maize plant)
155cm

12 mice standing on each
other's shoulders
98cm

ALL SHAPES AND SIZES

What are the longest, largest and most spectacular animals ever discovered?

Average adult male (UK) – standing up
1.74m

An eagle's nest (or eyrie) can be up to **5.5m** deep.

Saltwater crocodile –
6.3m

A baby blue whale is about
7m long –
the longest and largest baby in the natural world!

Reticulated python –
10m

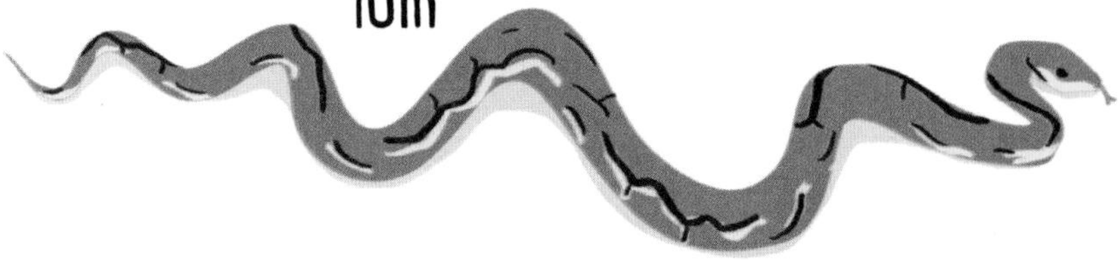

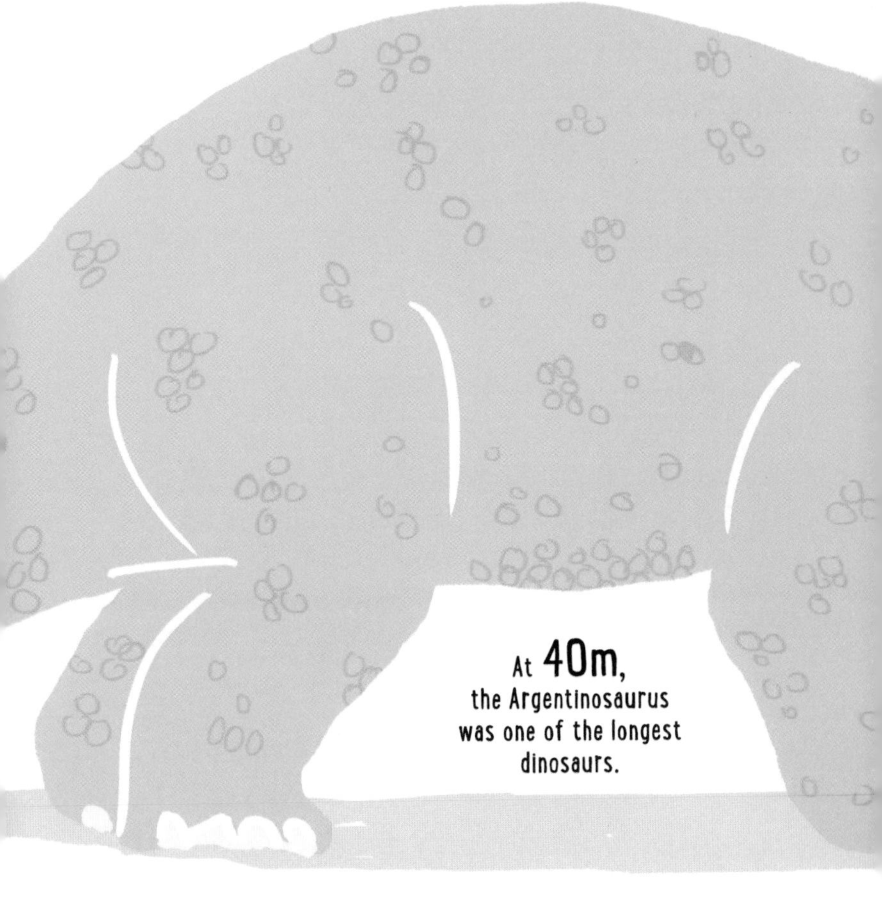

At **40m**,
the Argentinosaurus
was one of the longest
dinosaurs.

MORE! →

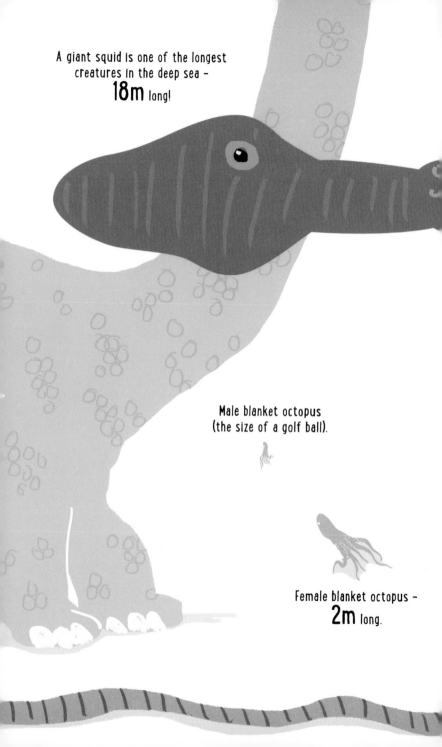

A giant squid is one of the longest creatures in the deep sea – **18m** long!

Male blanket octopus (the size of a golf ball).

Female blanket octopus – **2m** long.

An albatross has the longest wingspan of any bird **(3.5m)**.

A narwhal has the longest tooth in the animal kingdom – over **3m** long!

A rocket frog can jump **2m** (50 times its body length). This is like you being able to leap half way along a football pitch – in a single jump!

EVEN MORE! →

IT'LL NEVER WORK...

When two different species have a baby, it's known as a hybrid.
But what are the hybrids called?

A lion

A liger

When the father is a tiger and the mother a lion, this is known as a tigon.

A tiger

A zonkey

A zebra

A donkey

A male horse and a female zebra can also breed. Their baby is known as a hebra.

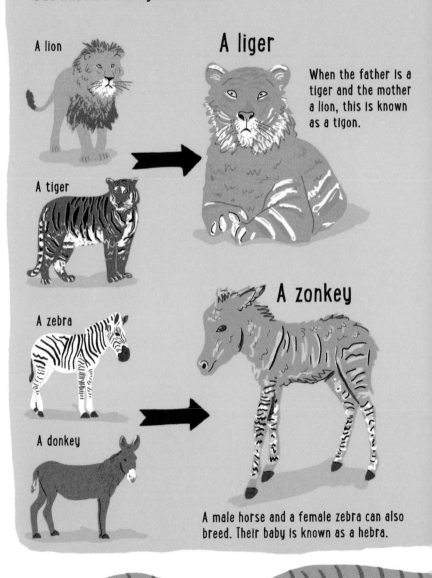

A false killer whale

A wholphin

A dolphin

A grizzly bear

A grolar bear

A polar bear

Where's my tail?

The longest animal ever discovered was a **55m** long bootlace worm!

COUNTDOWN

Things that happened as you read this sentence...*

Your body just made 30 million new cells.

12 babies were born.

Around 10,000 tonnes of water flowed over Niagara falls.

Earth flew 55 miles (90km) through space.

A humming bird flapped its wings 240 times.

The world's fastest car, the Ariel Atom, accelerated from 0 to 60 mph (100km/h).

Light from the Sun just travelled half a million miles towards Earth.

An area of Amazon rainforest the size of three football fields just got chopped down.

People used Google to search the internet almost half a million times.

Lightning struck the Earth 300 times.

*Assuming it took you three seconds to read it.

STEVE THE SQUIRREL'S SECRET TREASURE MAP

A squirrel can remember the location of up to 10,000 buried nuts!

FROM TINY ACORNS...
As well as the 10,000 they remember, squirrels also FORGET where HALF of their nuts are buried. Many of these grow into trees.

AIN'T NOTHING BUT A HOT DOG

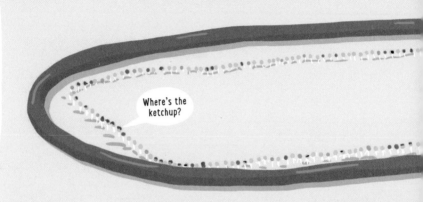

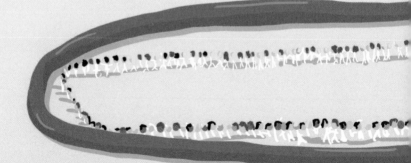

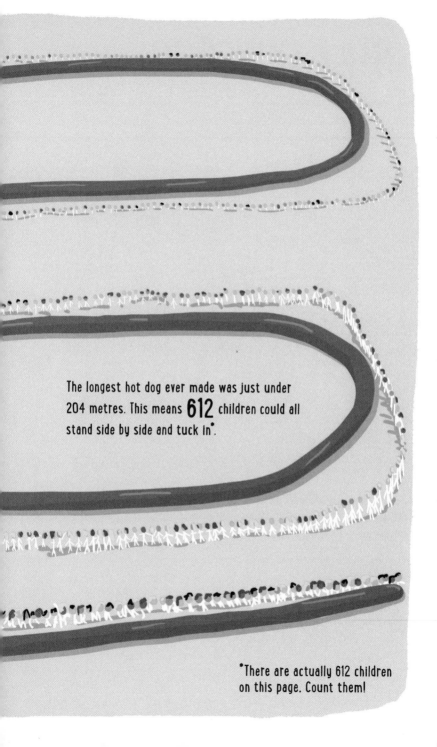

The longest hot dog ever made was just under 204 metres. This means **612** children could all stand side by side and tuck in.*

*There are actually 612 children on this page. Count them!

STILL HUNGRY?

Biggest ever pancake
15m wide

Biggest ever fruit cake
9m
460 baking trays were
used to bake it!

Longest ever kebab
8m

Biggest ever
hamburger
7.32m wide

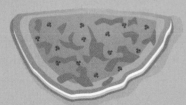

Biggest ever omelette
12m wide

A crowd of 3,500 people came to
watch the burger being cooked.
It took two hours.

Biggest ever doughnut
6m wide

Biggest ever chocolate bar
4m wide and **4m** long
It weighed nearly six tonnes.

Biggest ever pizza
37m wide*

*The pizza was made in Norwood, South Africa
by Norwood Hypermarket in 1990.

THUNDERSTRUCK

Roy Sullivan was a park ranger in the United States. He holds the world record as the person struck by lightning more times than any other human being. SEVEN TIMES.* But when, how and where?

1972
In a ranger station. Hair burnt off.

1969
While driving a truck. Eyebrows, eyelashes and some of his hair burnt off.

1977
Fishing. Head, chest and stomach burned.

1970
In his front yard. Left shoulder burnt.

1942
Hiding in a fire lookout tower. Strip burnt along his right leg.

1973
On patrol in the park. Left arm, left leg and right leg burnt. Left shoe blasted off.

1976
On patrol in the park. Ankle burnt.

*All seven lightning strikes were verified by doctors.

On another occasion, Roy Sullivan was almost hit by lightning while helping his wife hang out the washing in their back garden. But this time the lightning missed him and hit his wife instead.

FOLLOW YOUR NOSE

In 1925, a police dog picked up the scent of a sheep thief on the edge of the Great Karoo desert in South Africa. By following the scent, he finally caught up with the thief – 100 MILES LATER!

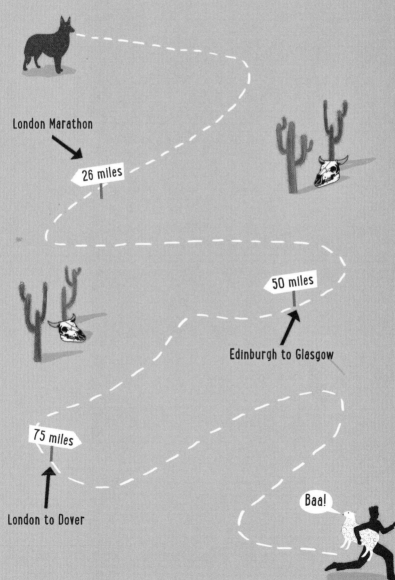

London Marathon

26 miles

50 miles

Edinburgh to Glasgow

75 miles

London to Dover

Baa!

WHAT A LIGHTWEIGHT!

How much would the average man weigh on different planets?
It depends on how big the planet is and how far he is from
the centre of the planet.

NEPTUNE   URANUS   SATURN   JUPITER   MARS

84Kg   67Kg   69Kg   28Kg   177Kg

= 25Kg

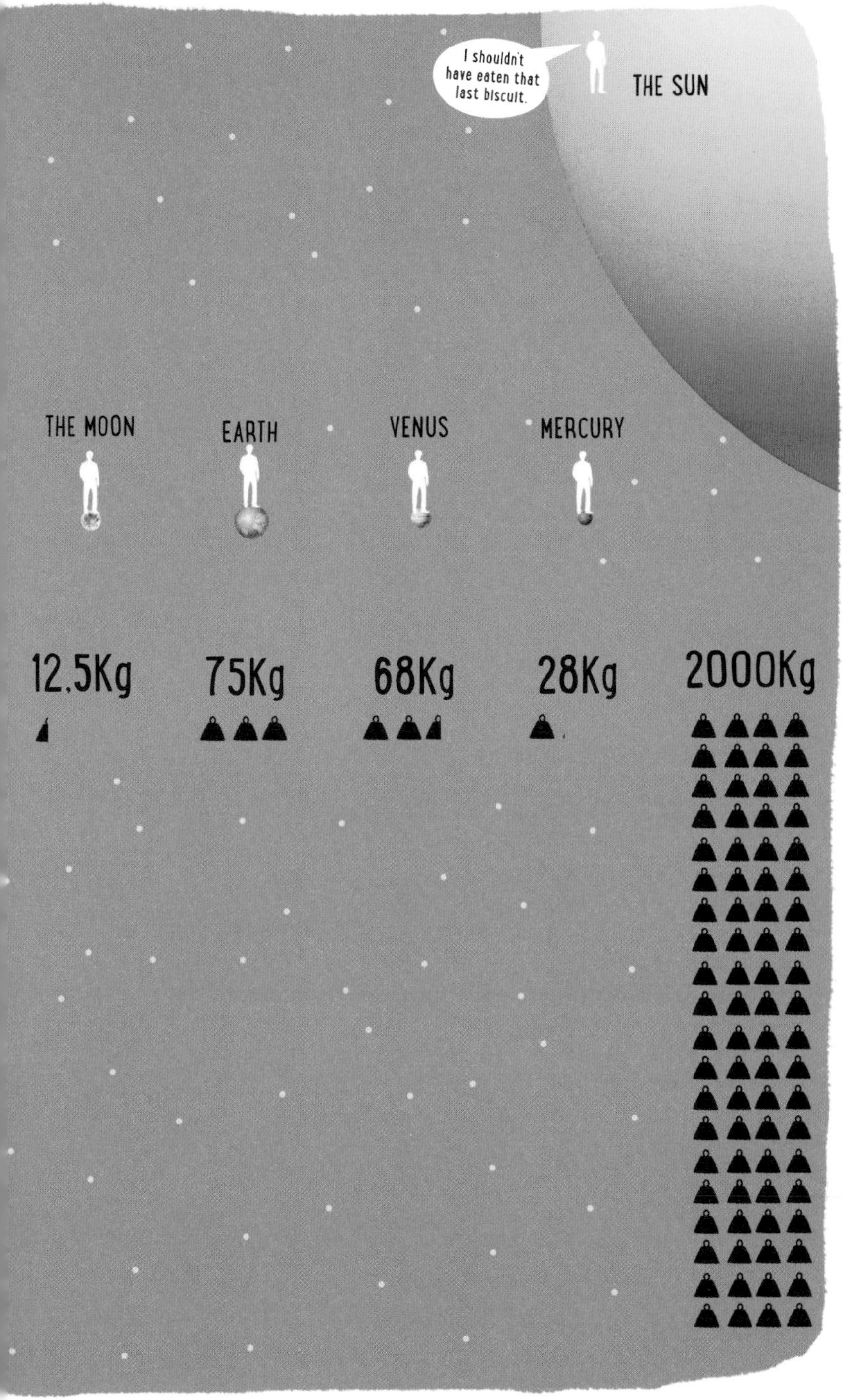
I shouldn't have eaten that last biscuit.
THE SUN
THE MOON
EARTH
VENUS
MERCURY
12,5Kg
75Kg
68Kg
28Kg
2000Kg

YOU COULDN'T MAKE IT UP...

The playwright William Shakespeare invented over 1,000 new words – more than any other author*. How many of these words do you know?

Eyeball

Puking

Belongings

Arch-villain

Elbow

Mountaineer

Manager

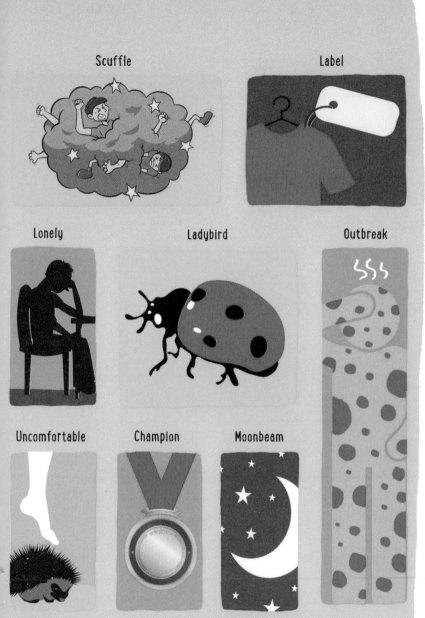

Scuffle

Label

Lonely

Ladybird

Outbreak

Uncomfortable

Champion

Moonbeam

*By invented, we mean he was the first person who ever wrote the words down or used them in public. People probably said them before – or they wouldn't have understood what Shakespeare was talking about.

ZOOM!

What's the zoom on your camera like? Bet it's not as good as a spy satellite. These cameras are 250 miles up in the sky, or biting round the Earth. And their zoom lens is INCREDIBLE.

ZOOMED OUT

ZOOMED IN

DRIVEN TO SUCCEED

A driver in Long Island, US has driven his car – a Volvo P1800S – THREE MILLION MILES. This is a world record! But how far is three million miles?

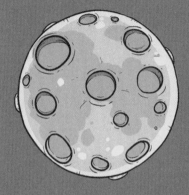

He could have driven to the Moon and back

6 TIMES.

The Maths:
Earth to Moon =

238,855 miles.

He could have driven round the Earth **120 TIMES.**

The Maths:
Circumference of Earth =

25,000 miles.

He could have driven across America coast-to-coast

1,434 times.

The Maths:
San Diego to Jacksonville =

2,092 miles.

LOUDER THAN WORDS

Using the right body language in the wrong place could land you in hot water...

Nodding	Bulgaria	Rest of the world
	No	Yes

Shaking hands	Asia	Rest of the world
	Very rude	Very friendly

Eye contact	US/Europe	South America, Middle East, Asia
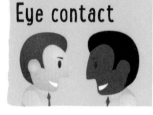	Very polite (I'm interested in what you're saying)	Very rude (I'm staring at you)

Eyes closed	US/Europe	China, Japan
	Very rude (I'm bored by what you're saying)	Very polite (I'm thinking hard about what you're saying)

HELLO MUM!

Which are the most popular days to make international phone calls?

 ## 1.Mother's Day
4th Sunday of Lent

 ## 2.New Year's Day
1st January

 ## 3.Valentine's Day
14th February
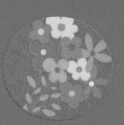

Mothers do OK for cards on Mother's Day too. Particularly when compared to fathers!

Number of cards sold in an average year:

Mother's Day	152 MILLION
Father's Day	95 MILLION

BANG BANG!

Fireworks come in all shapes and sizes...

The longest ever firework

⬅ **3.5km long** ➡

That's as long as 35 football pitches!

The biggest ever rocket

7m tall

The biggest ever Catherine wheel

32m wide

Some of the best-known firework shapes

The PEONY is the most common type of firework. It's named after the famous flower.

The WILLOW has long burning stars that make the firework look like a weeping willow.

The PALM bursts with large trails, making the firework look like a palm tree.

The DIADEM has a central cluster of stars that don't move, making the firework look like a crown.

MADE IN CHINA

90% of the world's fireworks are made in China.

Boo!

More than half of the world's fireworks are made in ONE PLACE in China – Liuyang.

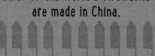

The Chinese invented fireworks in around 600 AD. They were originally designed to scare off evil sprits.

LET'S GET ROLLING

Ever wondered where you can find the world's longest or fastest roller coaster?

139m

Tate Modern,
London
99m

St Paul's Cathedral,
111m

Big Ben
96m

Ferrari Enzo
0-60 in 3.14 seconds

Formula Rossa rollercoaster, Abu Dhabi
0-60 in 2 seconds

The longest roller coaster

The roller coaster in Nagashima Spa Land, Japan is 2.48km long.

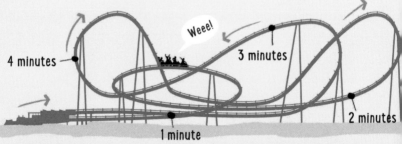

Weee!

4 minutes

3 minutes

1 minute

2 minutes

It takes over four minutes to get to the end. If you started boiling an egg when you got on, it would be ready to eat by the time you got off!

The tallest roller coaster

Kingda Ka in the United States is currently the tallest roller coaster in the world. It is 139m tall with a 127m drop.

127m

Porsche 911 Turbo
0-60 in 2.7 seconds

Ariel Atom V8
0-60 in 2.3 seconds

ZOOM!
ZOOM!

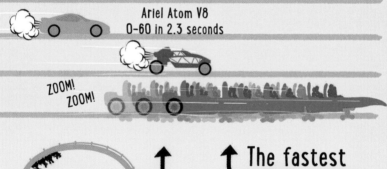

The fastest roller coaster

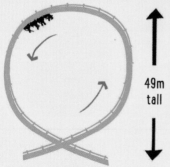

49m
tall

Scale

The tallest vertical loop roller coaster
Passengers on the full throttle roller coaster, California, USA.

NO WAY BACK

GOING...
1,000–5,000 left in the wild

Giant panda

Tiger

Galapagos penguin

Ganges river dolphin

GOING...
Fewer than 1,000 left in the wild

Mountain gorilla

Yangtze finless porpoise

Black-footed ferret

Mekong giant catfish

GONE
Extinct

Irish elk
These animals were 2m tall, but their incredible antlers measured 3.6m tip to tip.

Elephant bird
At 3m, these huge birds were twice the size of a man. Extinct since the 1700s.

Steller's sea cow
This amazing sea creature was 9m long and weighed around 10 tonnes.

We all know that dinosaurs are extinct. But there are animals that used to share the planet with humans – and now they are gone forever. What were these animals and which animals may soon be joining them?

Sumatran elephant   Black rhino   African wild dog   Snow leopard

Vaquita porpoise   Cross river gorilla   Javan rhino   Amur leopard

As dead as a …

Passenger pigeon
In 1500 there were five billion passenger pigeons in the US. 400 years later, there were none.

Dodo
The most famous extinct animal of all lived on the island of Mauritius until humans killed or ate them all.

Quagga
This zebra-like animal had brown and white stripes on the front half of its body. Extinct since 1883.

LET'S GO

Latest figures show there are 1140 Lego bricks on this page,
Across the world, people buy this much Lego every SECOND!

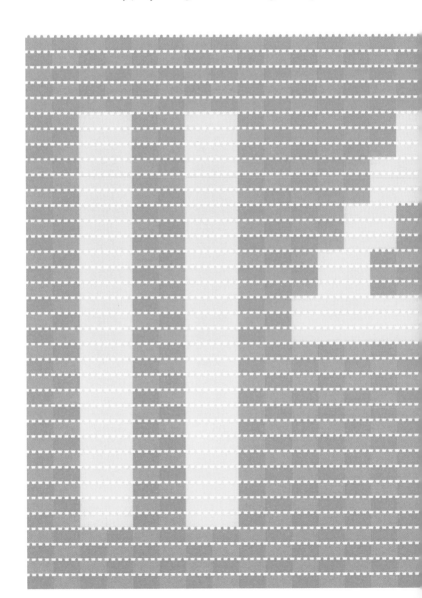

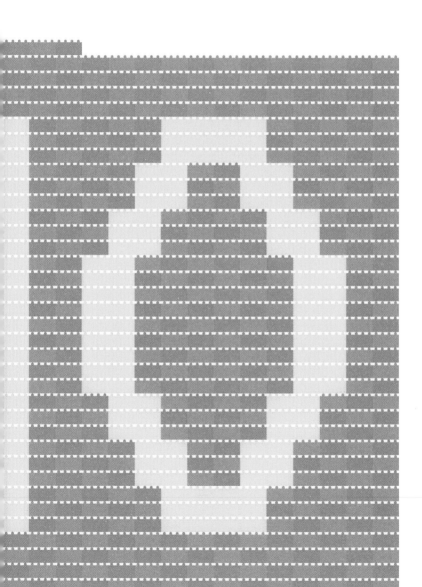

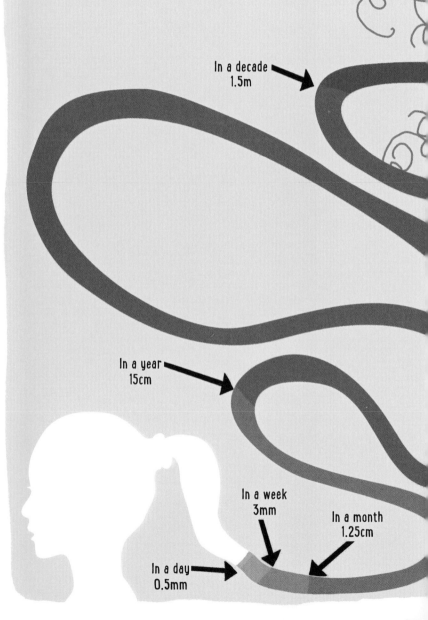

HAIR WE GO

How fast does the average person's hair grow?

In a decade
1.5m

In a year
15cm

In a week
3mm

In a month
1.25cm

In a day
0.5mm

In a lifetime
11m

TOO HOT TO HANDLE?

How hot is that chilli pepper? The Scoville scale can tell you...

Scoville heat units

2 million

1.5 million

Carolina Reaper
This fiery demon holds the record for the hottest chilli in the world. If you ate a whole one, you would almost certainly end up in hospital.

Infinity Chilli
This chilli is called 'Infinity' because of its 'never-ending' heat.

Dorset Naga
You can see some of these in the Eden Project in Cornwall. But they are kept behind a guard rail so people don't accidentally touch them.

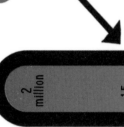

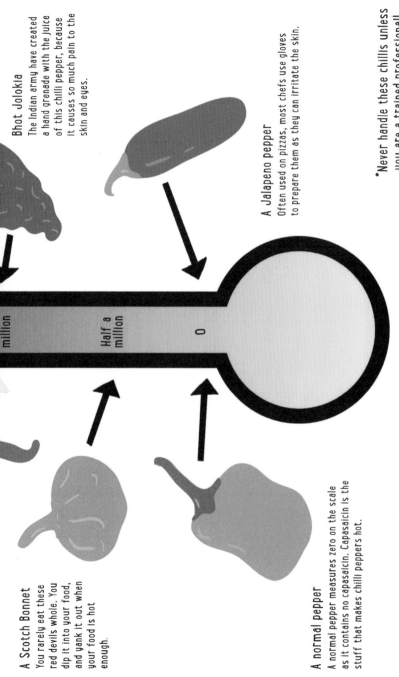

Bhot Jolokia
The Indian army have created a hand grenade with the juice of this chilli pepper, because it causes so much pain to the skin and eyes.

A Jalapeno pepper
Often used on pizzas, most chefs use gloves to prepare them as they can irritate the skin.

*Never handle these chillis unless you are a trained professional!

A Scotch Bonnet
You rarely eat these red devils whole. You dip it into your food, and yank it out when your food is hot enough.

A normal pepper
A normal pepper measures zero on the scale as it contains no capasaicin. Capasaicin is the stuff that makes chilli peppers hot.

million

Half a million

0

LEFT RIGHT LEFT RIGHT

In some countries – like the UK – you drive on the left. In others, they drive on the right. But what do MOST countries do?

54 countries drive on the left

142 countries drive on the right.

Arctic Ocean

North Pacific Ocean

North Atlantic Ocean

South Pacific Ocean

South Atlantic Ocean

North America

South America

Europe

Africa

Asia

Arctic Ocean

North Pacific Ocean

Indian Ocean

Oceania

LOOK WHO'S TALKING

What are the most widely-spoken languages in the world?
And how many people speak them?

Hello
English – 359 million

你好
Mandarin Chinese– 955 million

Hola
Spanish – 407 million

नमस्ते
Hindi – 311 million

مرحباً
Arabic – 293 million

Olá
Portuguese – 216 million

привет
Russian – 154 million

সলাম
Bengali – 206 million

TAKE TWO

Over HALF of the world speak TWO OR MORE languages
on a daily basis. How many languages can you speak?

OLDEST SPECIES

Some animal species have been around for
a very long time...

400 MILLION YEARS

Coelacanth (400 million years)
Previously thought to have been wiped
out 100 million years ago, coelacanths
were rediscovered in the 1930s and are
seen as a 'living fossil' as they haven't
changed in almost 400 million years.

**Lamprey
(360 million years)**
Many lampreys use their
sharp teeth to drill into the
flesh of other fish and drink
their blood. This ruthless way
of staying alive is one of the
reasons they've lasted for
over 300 million years.

150 MILLION YEARS

Frilled shark (150 million years)
This deep-water shark attacks like
a snake – coiling its body back
and then lunging forwards. Its long
jaws mean it can swallow prey whole.
It first appeared on Earth about the
same time as the Diplodocus –
but it's still here...

**Martialis Heureka Ant
(120 million years)**
These ants live deep underground
and are completely blind.

50 MILLION YEARS

100 MILLION YEARS

350 MILLION YEARS

300 MILLION YEARS

Horseshoe crab (200 million years)

Closely related to spiders and scorpions, these crabs have an incredibly hard shell and five pairs of legs – four of which have sharp claws at the tip.

Tadpole shrimp (220 million years)

Also described as living fossils, these shrimp live anywhere there is shallow water: rockpools, ponds, estuaries, streams, bogs or moorland. They also eat anything and everything.

250 MILLION YEARS

Tuatara (250 million years)

The tuatara is a New Zealand reptile with a frilled head. Like lizards, they can grow a new tail if a predator bites it off.

200 MILLION YEARS

Humans (200,000 years)

NOW

Snapping Turtle (40 million years)

Snapping turtles cannot hide in their shells like other turtles. This is why they 'snap' their jaws when attacked.

HOW DO YOU SLEEP?

Most people sleep in one of six positions. But which is the most common? And how do you sleep?

1 2 3 4 5 6

1. The Foetus
41% sleep in this position. These people are said to be tough on the outside but sensitive on the inside.

2. The Log
15% sleep in this position. These people are meant to be loyal and trusting.

3. The Yearner
13% sleep in this position. These people can be suspicious and stubborn – rarely changing their minds.

4. The Soldier
8% sleep in this position. These people are said to be quiet and reserved. They are also more likely to snore.

5. Freefall
7% sleep in this position. These people are outgoing and sociable, but don't like being told off or criticised.

6. The Starfish
5% sleep in this position. These people are open, friendly and helpful.

DREAM ON

When you're asleep, what do you dream about?
Here are the five most common dreams.

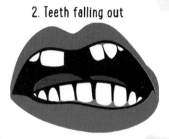

2. Teeth falling out

1. Being chased

4. Unprepared for an exam

3. Desperate for the toilet

5. Falling

WHAT RECORDS WILL YOU BREAK?

Just because you're young, it doesn't mean you can't be a record breaker.

At the age of 4, Dorothy Straight became the youngest person ever to pubish a book. It was called *How the World Began* and it also included Dorothy's pictures.

At 6, Luis Taner became the youngest ever TV presenter. His show *Cooking for Kids with Luis* was first aired in October 2004.

When he was 8, Kim Ung-Yong got a job with NASA. He also became a doctor at the age of 15.

4 5 6 7 8 9 10

By the age of 5. Eleanor Gamble had sunk a hole-in-one. She was playing in the 2010 Easter Pairs competition in Cambridge Lakes.

By the time she was 7, Connie Talbot had an album in the UK charts. It was called Over the Rainbow and it was released in 2007.

By the age of 9, Kishan Shrikanth had made a feature film. It was called *Care of Footpath* and it was about an orphaned boy who dreams of going to school.

At 10 years old, Tatum O'Neal won an Oscar. It was for a film called *Paper Moon*. The film also starred her father.

When he was 12, Sergey Karjakin became a chess grandmaster. He had started playing chess at the age of 5.

At the age of 14, Michael Perham sailed across the Atlantic Ocean by himself. His boat was called Cheeky Monkey.

11 12 13 14 15

By the age of 11, Thomas Gregory had swum the English Channel. It took him 11 hours and 54 minutes.

By the age of 13, Jordon Romero had climbed Mount Everest. This is the highest mountain in the world.

When he was 15, Reuben Noble-Lazarus become the youngest ever player in an English league match. He came on as a substitute for Barnsley in September 2008.

WHAT DID YOU CALL ME?

Kings and noblemen often have nicknames.
But who was called what?

Oi!

The FAT

| Alfonso II of Portugal | Charles III, Holy Roman Emperor | Conan II, Duke of Brittany | Henry I of Cyprus | Henry I of Navarre | Louis VI of France | Sancho I of Leon |

The MAD

| Charles VI of France | George III of Great Britain | Joanna of Castile | Ludwig II of Bavaria |

The BALD

| Charles II of France | Baldwin II, Count of Flanders | Idwal ab Anarawd of Gwynedd |

The DRUNKARD

Burp!

| Michael III, Byzantine Emperor | Selim II, Ottoman Emperor | Wenceslaus, King of the Romans |

The SILENT

Shh!

| Olav III of Norway | William I of Orange |

The QUARRELLER

Rarr!

| Frederick of Saxony | Louis X of France |

The UNLUCKY

| Arnulf III of Flanders | Henry III of Reuss |

NOTHING TO SEA HERE...

We know more about the surface of the Moon than we do about the deepest part of the ocean.

Number of people who've been in space[*]

534

Number of people who've climbed Everest

over

3000

Number of people who've been to the bottom of the ocean[**]

three

Don Walsh and Jacques Piccard made their journey in 1960. It took them five hours to reach the ocean bed and three hours and 15 minutes to get back.

The deepest part of the sea is called the Mariana Trench. Three people who have travelled there are Don Walsh, Jacques Piccard and James Cameron – director of the film *Titanic*.

[*] From 1961 to 2013.   [**] The Mariana Trench.

129 mm

10
10p piece

ACTUAL SIZE
Everything on these pages is exactly the same size as it is in real life.*

A dwarf lantern shark – the world's smallest shark

A bumblebee bat – the world's smallest mammal

*except for the baby kangaroo. all of the animals here are adults – their babies are even smaller!

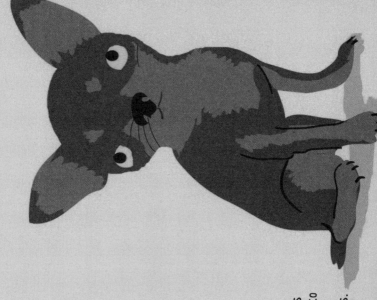

Milly, the world's smallest living dog

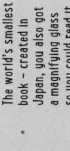

The world's smallest book – created in Japan, you also got a magnifying glass so you could read it.

The world's smallest colour TV screen. It was created in 2002.

Thiomargarita namibiensis – the largest bacteria in the world.

Smallest unicycle wheel. Peter Rosendahl rode this unicycle 5 metres in 2011.

Smallest dinosaur footprint. The exact species of dinosaur that made the print is not known.

Paedophryne amauensis– the world's smallest frog.

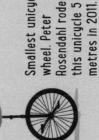

A baby kangaroo. The tiny joey crawls up its mother's belly and into her pouch, where it stays for nine months.

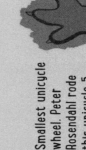

SEE YOU IN THREE DAYS...

This is how far you could travel in **three days** at different times in history on different types of transport.

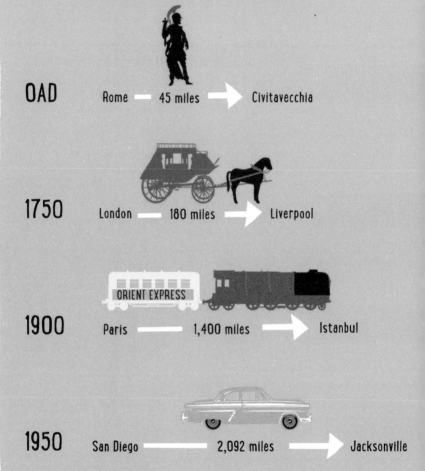

0AD   Rome — 45 miles → Civitavecchia

1750   London — 180 miles → Liverpool

1900   Paris — 1,400 miles → Istanbul

1950   San Diego — 2,092 miles → Jacksonville

2000   Earth

238.855 miles

THE RED PLANET

A trip to Mars would take us between five and nine months. That's roughly how long it would have taken a Roman army to march from Rome to London.

The Moon

OIL

The oil that we pump out of the ground is used – most famously – as fuel for our cars. But there are also hundreds of other things – from clothes to medicine – that wouldn't exist without this incredible substance. Here are a few of them...

GAMES AND LEISURE

Golf ball

Balloon

Fishing line

CD

Tennis racket

Paint brush

Fishing line

Glue

Football

Goggles

Crayon

Sponge

Tablet

Bottle

HEALTH

Helmet

Life ring

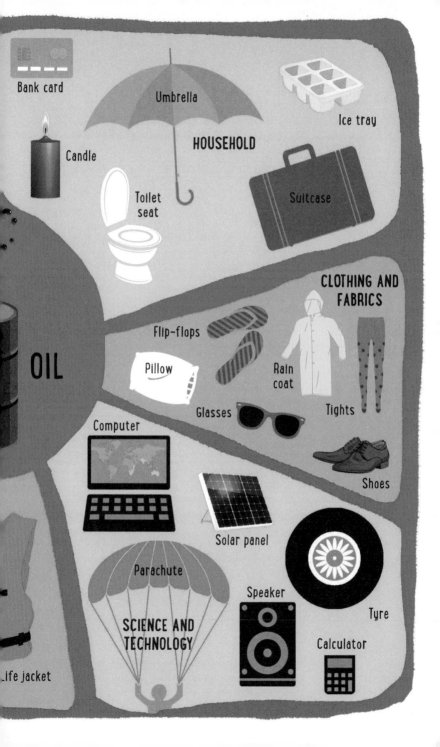

TOTALLY CRUSHED

Meet Albert the Alien. He comes from the Planet Sparg – where atmospheric pressure is 15,000psi (pounds per square inch). So nothing on Earth can possibly crush him. Can it?

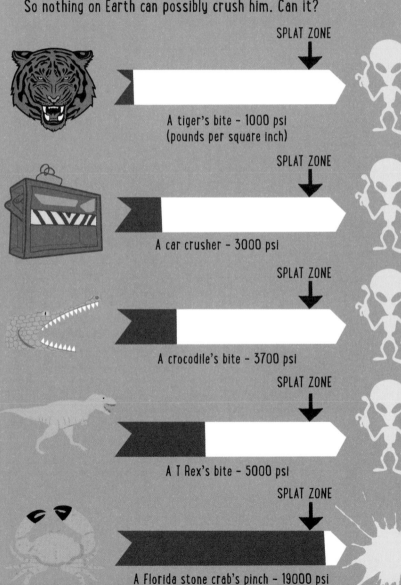

SPLAT ZONE

A tiger's bite – 1000 psi
(pounds per square inch)

SPLAT ZONE

A car crusher – 3000 psi

SPLAT ZONE

A crocodile's bite – 3700 psi

SPLAT ZONE

A T Rex's bite – 5000 psi

SPLAT ZONE

A Florida stone crab's pinch – 19000 psi

SNOWFALL*

In 2011, Tomas Bergemalm reportedly broke the record for the highest freefall cliff jump. In other words, he skied off a cliff without a parachute, relying on the snow to cushion his fall.

As he fell, Tomas reached speeds of 125mph.

183m fall

Big Ben – 96m

Statue of Liberty – 93m

When Jamie Pierre performed a 100m freefall jump in 2006, his landing made a 3m-wide crater.

He was completely unharmed by the jump, although he ended up with a cut lip from a shovel when his friends dug him out of the hole.

*These are world records and should never be attempted.

SEE YOU ONLINE

In just over a decade, the whole world has got used to living online.

Average Google searches
per day

5.9 billion

60 million

2000

2013

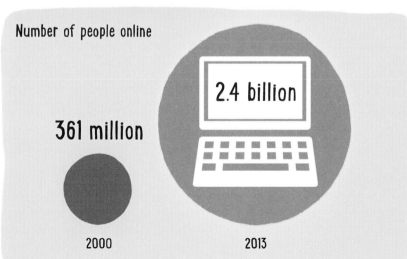

Number of people online

2.4 billion

361 million

2000

2013

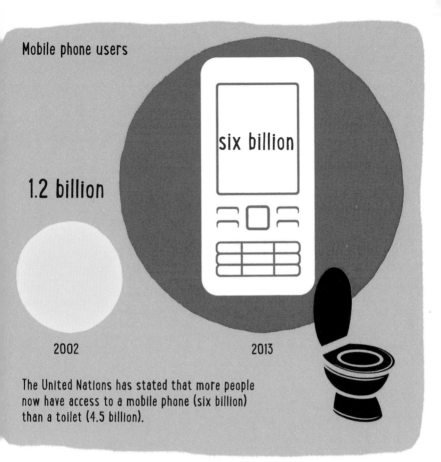

Mobile phone users

1.2 billion
2002

six billion
2013

The United Nations has stated that more people now have access to a mobile phone (six billion) than a toilet (4.5 billion).

Number of websites

1	130	100,000	162 million	670 million
1990	1993	1996	2008	2013

In 1990, there was just one website: info.cern.ch. It was set up by the inventor of the World Wide Web, Tim Berners-Lee. The website still exists.

SUPERBUGS

Insects and arthropods are creepy enough now, but in prehistoric times, they were even bigger and ever badder!

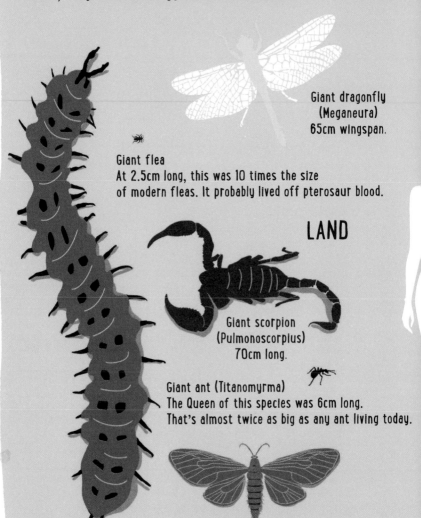

Giant dragonfly
(Meganeura)
65cm wingspan.

Giant flea
At 2.5cm long, this was 10 times the size of modern fleas. It probably lived off pterosaur blood.

LAND

Giant scorpion
(Pulmonoscorpius)
70cm long.

Giant ant (Titanomyrma)
The Queen of this species was 6cm long.
That's almost twice as big as any ant living today.

Giant centipede
(Arthropleura)
2.6m.

Giant flying extinct moth-like thing
(Mazothairos)
55cm wingspan.

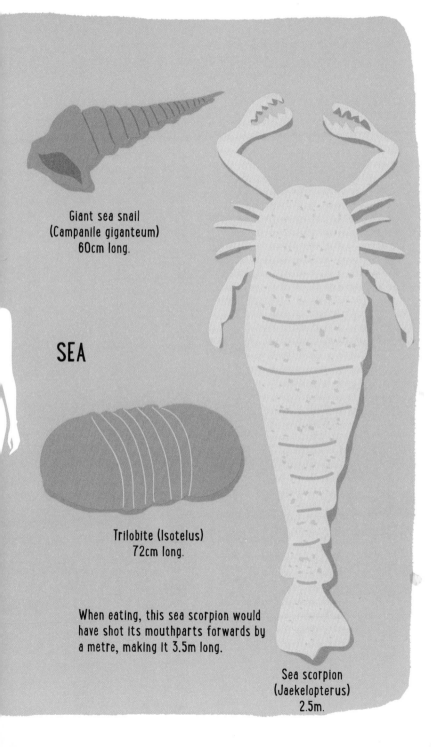

Giant sea snail
(Campanile giganteum)
60cm long.

SEA

Trilobite (Isotelus)
72cm long.

When eating, this sea scorpion would
have shot its mouthparts forwards by
a metre, making it 3.5m long.

Sea scorpion
(Jaekelopterus)
2.5m.

SOURCES

This book would not have been possible without a wide range of other books, not to mention magazines, websites, tweets and TV shows. Here are some of the best.

BRILLIANT BOOKS:
Knowledge Encyclopedia (Dorling Kindersley, 2013)
Guinness World Records (Guinness World Records, 2013)
Children's Encyclopaedia of Animals (Dorling Kindersley, 2009)
The Natural World by Jon Richards and Ed Simkins (Owlkids, 2012)
Ripley's Believe It or Not 2014 by Ripley Publishing (Random House, 2013)
5000 Awesome Facts (About Everything) (National Geographic, 2012)
That's Gross! by Crispin Boyer (National Geographic, 2012)
Top 10 of Everything by Caroline Ash and Alexander Ash (Hamlyn, 2011)
The Big Book of Knowledge (Parragon, 2010)
How It Works Book of Junior Science (Imagine Publishing, 2013)
1227 QI Facts to Blow Your Socks Off – Kindle Edition by John Lloyd and John Mitchinson (Faber and Faber, 2012).
1339 QI Facts to Make Your Jaw Drop – Kindle Edition by John Lloyd and John Mitchinson (Faber and Faber, 2013)
Plus the QI TV show and the QI Elves on Twitter
Boys' Miscellany by Martin Oliver (Buster Books, 2012)
Bumbelievable: The Bumper Book of Facts (Macmillan, 2013)
The How it Works Book of Amazing Answers to Curious Questions – Kindle Edition (Imagine Publishing, 2011)
Hmm... I did not know that by A.P. Holiday – Kindle Editon (Haymaker, 2011)
Awesome Facts (Igloo, 2009)
You Won't Believe It But... (Igloo, 2010)

WONDERFUL WEBSITES:
www.britannica.com/
http://kids.britannica.com/
www.guinnessworldrecords.com
www.nationalgeographic.com/
qi.com
uber-facts.com
http://www.newscientist.com/
http://www.nasa.gov/
http://www.lookandlearn.com/
http://www.technologyreview.com/
Newspaper websites: Guardian, Independent, Huffington Post, Telegraph and Daily Mail
http://www.bbc.co.uk/news
And, of course, Google.